QUICKBOOKS ONLI... ...
BEGINNERS TO ADVANCED
USERS

All-in-One Guide for Entrepreneurs and Small Business Owners. From Setting Up Your Books to Automating Workflows, Taxes, and Financial Reports.

Elliot Gray

CHAPTER FIFTEEN

BONUS SECTION

CONCLUSION

INTRODUCTION

This guide is designed to be your trusted companion on the journey from understanding the basics of QuickBooks Online to mastering advanced features that empower you to run your business more efficiently.

Who Is This Book For?

Whether you're an entrepreneur starting a new venture, a freelancer managing your own finances, a small business owner juggling multiple tasks, or even an accountant seeking a streamlined approach for your clients, this ebook has been crafted with you in mind. It speaks directly to anyone who wants to transform their financial management by leveraging the power of cloud accounting.

How to Use This Guide Effectively

This book is structured to grow with you. We begin with the fundamentals—understanding why QuickBooks Online is the go-to solution for modern business accounting, setting up your account, and configuring your company settings. As you progress, you'll explore essential topics such as creating a tailored Chart of Accounts, managing sales and expenses, tracking inventory, and even handling payroll. Intermediate chapters delve into banking, reconciliation, and project costing, while advanced sections unlock the secrets to customizing reports, automating workflows, and optimizing tax management. Each chapter is designed to be actionable and easy to follow, with clear explanations, practical examples, and step-by-step instructions. Feel free to jump to the sections most relevant to your current needs or read through the guide sequentially for a comprehensive understanding.

A Glimpse at the Content

- **Part 1** starts by explaining *Why QuickBooks Online?* with an emphasis on the benefits of cloud accounting, a comparison of available plans, and a deep dive into the key features that make this tool indispensable.

- **Part 2** guides you through setting up your account, choosing the right plan, and navigating your dashboard, as well as configuring your company settings—from setting up your business profile to customizing preferences and branding your account.

- **Part 3** gets into the nuts and bolts: understanding your Chart of Accounts, managing your sales, customer interactions, expenses, vendors, and even tracking inventory.

- **Part 4** explores more advanced topics like payroll setup, banking automation, job costing, and in-depth reporting, budgeting, forecasting, and automation of workflows.

- **Part 5** offers power-user insights, from time-saving tips and keyboard shortcuts to common pitfalls, data security, and best practices for managing user permissions.

Your Exclusive Bonuses

To further enhance your experience and provide additional value, this guide includes three exclusive bonuses:

- **Bonus 1: Quick Reference Cheat Sheet** – A handy compilation of shortcuts and workflow tips that you can refer to at a glance when you need that extra bit of guidance.

- **Bonus 2: 30-Day QuickBooks Setup Challenge** – A daily checklist that walks you through every step of setting up and mastering QuickBooks Online, ensuring you stay on track and make the most out of each feature.

- **Bonus 3: Exclusive Templates Pack** – Gain access to professionally designed invoice templates, sample charts of accounts, and budget templates that can be customized to fit your unique business needs.

As you embark on this journey through the world of QuickBooks Online, remember that each chapter is crafted to provide clarity and practical insights that make complex tasks manageable. By the end of this guide, you'll not only have the confidence to use QuickBooks Online like a pro but also the tools and tips to optimize your business operations for success.

Let's dive in and unlock the full potential of QuickBooks Online together!

CHAPTER ONE

Why QuickBooks Online?

Welcome to the first chapter of your journey toward mastering QuickBooks Online! In this chapter, we'll explore why QuickBooks Online (QBO) is the modern solution for managing your business finances, and how it can transform the way you handle accounting. Whether you're new to accounting or looking to upgrade your current system, understanding the benefits of cloud accounting, comparing QBO plans, and discovering its standout features will show you why this tool is a game-changer.

The Benefits of Cloud Accounting

Imagine having your entire accounting system accessible from anywhere, at any time, and on any device. That's the promise of cloud accounting, and QuickBooks Online brings this promise to life. Here are some key advantages:

- **Accessibility and Flexibility:** With QBO, you no longer need to be tied to a specific computer or office. Whether you're at home, in the office, or on the go, you can log in securely and manage your finances. This flexibility means you can keep your finger on the pulse of your business, even if you're traveling or working remotely.

- **Real-Time Data and Collaboration:** QuickBooks Online continuously updates your financial data. This real-time insight allows you to make informed decisions quickly. Plus, if you work with an accountant or a team, multiple users can access the same information simultaneously, ensuring everyone is on the same page.

- **Automatic Updates and Security:** Cloud-based software like QBO is always evolving. You benefit from the latest features and security enhancements without the hassle of manual updates. Your data is stored in secure servers, with regular backups and robust encryption, giving you peace of mind that your financial information is safe.

- **Cost-Effective and Scalable:** For small business owners and entrepreneurs, every dollar counts. QuickBooks Online offers various subscription plans to match your business size and needs, helping you avoid the high upfront costs of traditional accounting software. As your business grows, QBO can scale with you, accommodating your expanding needs without a costly overhaul.

Comparing QuickBooks Online Plans

Choosing the right plan is crucial to getting the most out of QuickBooks Online. Here's a brief overview to help you navigate the options:

- **Simple Start:** Ideal for solopreneurs and very small businesses, this plan covers basic accounting needs such as invoicing, expense tracking, and receipt capture. It's a great way to dip your toes into cloud accounting without feeling overwhelmed.

- **Essentials:** This plan builds on the Simple Start features and adds tools for managing bills and tracking time. If you're a growing business that needs to handle more complex transactions and keep better tabs on project costs, Essentials offers a well-rounded solution.

- **Plus:** Perfect for small businesses that require robust inventory tracking and project profitability insights, the Plus plan includes all the features of Essentials plus advanced capabilities like inventory management and budgeting. It's designed for those who need a bit more control and detail in their financial reporting.

- **Advanced:** Tailored for businesses that are scaling quickly, the Advanced plan delivers premium features such as enhanced custom reporting, dedicated customer support, and deeper insights into business performance. If you're looking to push the boundaries and fully harness QuickBooks Online's potential, this is the plan to consider.

When choosing a plan, think about your current needs as well as your future growth. The flexibility of QBO means you can always start with a basic plan and upgrade as your business evolves.

Key Features You'll Love

QuickBooks Online is packed with features designed to simplify accounting and empower you to run your business more efficiently. Here are some of the standout features that you're sure to appreciate:

- **User-Friendly Dashboard:** The intuitive interface makes it easy to navigate between different functions. From viewing your cash flow at a glance to drilling down into specific transactions, the dashboard is designed with ease of use in mind.

- **Automated Workflows:** Say goodbye to repetitive manual tasks. QBO automates many processes such as recurring invoices, bank reconciliations, and even payment reminders. This automation saves you time and reduces the likelihood of human error.

- **Robust Reporting:** QuickBooks Online offers a range of customizable reports. Whether you need a quick snapshot of your profit and loss, a detailed balance sheet, or a cash flow report, QBO provides the data you need to make smart financial decisions.

- **Seamless Integrations:** One of the most powerful aspects of QBO is its ability to integrate with other business tools. From CRM systems to payroll services and third-party apps like Zapier and Gusto, these integrations help create a cohesive and efficient business ecosystem.

- **Mobile Accessibility:** In today's fast-paced world, being able to manage your business on the go is a huge advantage. The mobile app for QuickBooks Online ensures that you have access to all your essential functions right from your smartphone or tablet.

- **Continuous Innovation:** QuickBooks Online is regularly updated with new features and improvements. This commitment to innovation means that you're always working with state-of-the-art tools that keep you ahead of the curve in financial management.

Wrapping Up

In this chapter, we've explored why QuickBooks Online is more than just a digital ledger—it's a powerful, flexible, and secure tool designed to adapt to the unique needs of your business. By embracing cloud accounting, you not only gain real-time insights and enhanced collaboration but also a scalable solution that grows with your business.

In the chapters ahead, we'll delve deeper into setting up your account, configuring your business settings, and leveraging the many features that make QuickBooks Online an indispensable asset. With a clear understanding of the "why" behind QBO, you're now ready to jump into the "how" and start transforming your business financials like a pro.

Let's move forward together, confident that you've chosen a tool that's designed to support your business every step of the way!

CHAPTER TWO

Setting Up Your Account

Now that you understand why QuickBooks Online is a powerful tool for your business, it's time to get started by setting up your account. In this chapter, we'll walk you through the initial steps of joining the QuickBooks Online community, selecting the right plan for your business, and familiarizing yourself with the user-friendly dashboard. By the end, you'll feel confident and ready to dive into your financial data.

Signing Up for QuickBooks Online

The journey to a more organized and efficient way of handling your business finances starts with a simple sign-up process. Here's how to get started:

- **Easy Registration:** QuickBooks Online offers a streamlined sign-up process designed with beginners in mind. All you need is an internet connection, your business details, and a willingness to embrace a modern accounting solution.

- **Guided Onboarding:** Once you sign up, QuickBooks Online walks you through an onboarding process that sets the stage for your new financial management system.

This process includes prompts to input key business information, helping tailor the platform to your specific needs.

- **Getting Secure:** As you register, you'll also set up secure login credentials. QuickBooks Online takes data security seriously, ensuring that your sensitive financial information is protected through robust encryption and regular updates.

Remember, the initial sign-up is just the first step in your journey. With a few clicks, you're opening the door to a world of efficient financial management.

Choosing the Right Plan

QuickBooks Online is built to grow with you, offering a variety of plans that cater to different business sizes and needs. Here's what you need to consider when choosing your plan:

- **Understanding Your Needs:** Before selecting a plan, take a moment to assess your business requirements. Are you a solopreneur with straightforward invoicing needs, or do you require advanced features like inventory tracking and detailed reporting? Understanding your needs will help you choose the plan that best aligns with your current operations and future growth.

- **Plan Options Overview:**

  o **Simple Start:** Perfect for those who are just beginning or have minimal accounting needs. This plan covers basic tasks like invoicing, expense tracking, and receipt capture.

  o **Essentials:** A step up from Simple Start, Essentials adds bill management and time tracking—ideal for growing businesses that need a bit more control.

  o **Plus:** This plan offers robust features including inventory tracking and budgeting, making it suitable for businesses that need comprehensive financial oversight.

  o **Advanced:** Designed for larger or rapidly growing businesses, Advanced provides premium features such as custom reporting and priority support, ensuring you have the tools to take your financial management to the next level.

- **Future-Proofing Your Business:** The beauty of QuickBooks Online is that you can always start small and upgrade as your business evolves. This flexibility means you won't be locked into a plan that no longer meets your needs, and you can expand your capabilities as your business grows.

Take your time evaluating these options. The right plan will empower you to manage your finances more efficiently and set a strong foundation for your business success.

Navigating the Dashboard

After signing up and choosing the perfect plan, the next step is familiarizing yourself with the QuickBooks Online dashboard. Think of the dashboard as the command center for your business's financial health.

- **A User-Friendly Interface:** The dashboard is designed with simplicity in mind. With clear, intuitive menus and real-time data displays, you'll quickly be able to see key financial metrics like cash flow, expenses, and profit at a glance.

- **Customizable Views:** One of the great features of the dashboard is its flexibility. You can customize the layout to highlight the information that matters most to you. Whether it's your recent transactions, upcoming bills, or performance reports, everything is just a few clicks away.

- **Quick Access to Essential Functions:** The dashboard provides easy navigation to important areas such as invoicing, expense tracking, and reporting. Its organized layout ensures you're never overwhelmed, making routine tasks both efficient and manageable.

- **Interactive Elements:** Many of the dashboard's components are interactive. For example, clicking on a financial summary might open up a more detailed report, allowing you to drill down into the specifics of your numbers. This interactivity helps turn raw data into actionable insights.

Take some time to explore the dashboard after your initial setup. Experiment with its features, adjust the settings, and start to build a view that best supports your daily operations.

Wrapping Up

Setting up your QuickBooks Online account is a foundational step toward transforming the way you manage your business finances. By signing up, choosing the right plan, and navigating your dashboard, you're establishing a solid platform that will grow with your business. This chapter has provided you with the essential steps and insights needed to get started confidently. In the next chapters, we'll build on this foundation by diving into company settings, managing your chart of accounts, and much more.

Welcome to a new era of simplified, efficient, and empowering financial management. Your journey with QuickBooks Online has just begun!

CHAPTER THREE

Configuring Your Company Settings

Welcome to the next step in your QuickBooks Online journey—configuring your company settings. This chapter is all about making QuickBooks Online feel like your own. We'll guide you through setting up your business profile, customizing your preferences, and adding your logo and branding so that your financial management tool truly reflects your business identity.

Setting Up Your Business Profile

Your business profile is the digital representation of your company within QuickBooks Online. It's where you enter essential details that define your business and influence how your financial information is managed. Here's how to make your profile work for you:

- **Enter Accurate Information:** Start by filling in your company's name, address, contact details, and industry. This might seem basic, but accurate details are crucial for generating invoices, tax forms, and other official documents.

- **Define Your Business Structure:** Whether you're a sole proprietor, partnership, or incorporated business, selecting the correct structure helps QuickBooks tailor its features to your needs. This information also plays a role when setting up your tax configurations later on.

- **Update as You Grow:** As your business evolves, don't forget to revisit your profile. Keeping your details current ensures that every part of QuickBooks—from customer invoices to vendor payments—remains aligned with your real-world operations.

By setting up a comprehensive business profile, you're laying a strong foundation that ensures all your financial data is accurate and personalized.

Customizing Preferences

QuickBooks Online offers a variety of customizable preferences that allow you to tailor the system to your unique business needs. This flexibility is one of the key strengths of cloud accounting, enabling you to work in the way that suits you best.

- **Currency Settings:** If you work with multiple currencies or have an international client base, setting up the correct currency preferences is essential. QuickBooks Online lets you choose your home currency and, if needed, enable multi-currency functionality to manage international transactions smoothly.

- **Tax Year and Reporting Preferences:** Configure your tax year and other fiscal details to ensure that your financial reports and tax forms are accurate. This step is vital for aligning your accounting cycles with your local tax laws and business cycles. Whether you follow a calendar or fiscal year, setting these preferences correctly from the start saves you from potential headaches during tax season.

- **General Preferences:** Dive into settings that control how QuickBooks handles dates, reminders, and other operational details. Adjust settings related to invoices, payments, and reminders to suit your business's workflow. For instance, you might want to set up automatic payment reminders or customize how often your reports update.

Taking the time to customize your preferences means that QuickBooks Online becomes a tailored tool—working the way you work, rather than forcing you to adapt to its defaults.

Adding Your Logo and Branding

Branding is more than just a visual appeal; it's an integral part of how you present your business to clients, vendors, and partners.

QuickBooks Online offers easy options to incorporate your brand identity into your financial documents and reports.

- **Upload Your Logo:** Your logo is the visual cornerstone of your brand. Uploading it into QuickBooks Online ensures that your invoices, estimates, and other documents look professional and consistent. It adds a personal touch that reassures clients they're dealing with a well-organized business.

- **Customize Colors and Styles:** Beyond your logo, you can adjust color schemes and design elements to match your brand. Consistency in colors and styles across your communications not only reinforces your brand identity but also creates a cohesive look that enhances customer trust.

- **Personalize Your Invoices and Estimates:** Use the customization features in QuickBooks Online to create invoices and estimates that reflect your brand's personality. From choosing fonts and layouts to adding a personalized message, every detail can be fine-tuned so that your documents are a natural extension of your business's visual identity.

By investing a little time in branding, you transform your financial documents from plain transactions into extensions of your business's story.

Wrapping Up

Configuring your company settings in QuickBooks Online is about more than just inputting data—it's about making the platform truly yours. By setting up a detailed business profile, customizing your preferences, and adding your logo and branding, you're creating an environment that not only manages your finances efficiently but also represents your business accurately and professionally.

As you move forward, these settings will serve as the backbone of your financial management system, ensuring that everything from everyday transactions to year-end reports aligns with your business's identity and goals. In the next chapters, we'll delve deeper into the nuts and bolts of your accounting system, building on the personalized foundation you've just established.

Now that you've configured your company settings, you're one step closer to mastering QuickBooks Online. Enjoy the journey—each configuration choice you make today sets the stage for smoother, more efficient operations tomorrow!

CHAPTER FOUR

Chart of Accounts Explained

Welcome to Chapter 4, where we demystify one of the most critical components of your QuickBooks Online setup: the Chart of Accounts. In this chapter, we'll break down what the Chart of Accounts is, why it matters for your business, and how to set it up and customize it to suit your unique financial needs.

What Is the Chart of Accounts and Why It Matters

Imagine your Chart of Accounts as the backbone of your accounting system. It's a comprehensive list of every account you use to organize and track your business's financial transactions. Here's why it's so essential:

- **A Clear Financial Roadmap:** The Chart of Accounts categorizes your income, expenses, assets, liabilities, and equity. This structure creates a clear roadmap of your financial health, making it easier to see where your money is coming from and where it's going.

- **Accurate Financial Reporting:** Every transaction you record is linked to an account in your Chart of Accounts. This linkage ensures that your financial statements—like your profit and loss report and balance sheet—are accurate, detailed, and meaningful. Accurate reporting is vital for making informed decisions and staying on top of your business finances.

- **Streamlined Tax Preparation:** A well-organized Chart of Accounts simplifies tax time. When your accounts are neatly categorized, gathering the necessary information for tax filings becomes less daunting, helping you avoid errors and potential penalties.

- **Enhanced Business Insights:** By customizing your Chart of Accounts, you can tailor your financial reporting to highlight the metrics that matter most to your business. Whether you want to track revenue streams, monitor expenses, or analyze profit margins, a well-structured chart offers the insights you need to drive growth.

Setting Up and Customizing Your Accounts

Now that you understand its importance, let's dive into the practical steps of setting up and customizing your Chart of Accounts in QuickBooks Online. The goal here is to create a system that not only meets standard accounting requirements but also aligns with your specific business operations.

1. Getting Started with the Default Chart

- **Built-In Categories:** QuickBooks Online comes with a default Chart of Accounts that includes a broad range of categories. These defaults are designed to cover the basics for most businesses, from income and expenses to assets and liabilities.

- **Review and Understand:** Before making any changes, take some time to review the default accounts. This review will help you understand how your financial transactions are being categorized right out of the box.

2. Customizing Your Chart of Accounts

- **Adding New Accounts:** Every business is unique. If the default chart doesn't cover every aspect of your operations, you can easily add new accounts. For instance, if you have a specialized revenue stream or a unique expense category, create an account that reflects that.

- **Editing Existing Accounts:** You may find that some default accounts need to be renamed or adjusted to better fit your business model. Customizing account names and descriptions ensures clarity when you're reviewing financial reports or working with your accountant.

- **Deleting or Inactivating Unnecessary Accounts:** To keep your Chart of Accounts streamlined, remove any accounts that are not relevant to your business. If you're not ready to permanently delete an account, consider inactivating it so it no longer appears in your active lists.

3. Organizing for Better Financial Management

- **Group Similar Accounts:** Organize your accounts into logical groups. For example, group all operating expenses together or separate cost of goods sold from general administrative expenses. This grouping makes it easier to analyze your financial statements and spot trends.

- **Set Up Sub-Accounts:** For more detailed tracking, use sub-accounts. Sub-accounts allow you to break down a main account into smaller, more specific categories. For example, under a general "Expenses" account, you might have sub-accounts for utilities, rent, and office supplies.

- **Regular Maintenance:** As your business evolves, your Chart of Accounts should evolve with it. Regularly review and update your accounts to ensure they accurately reflect your current operations. This ongoing maintenance helps avoid clutter and maintains the precision of your financial records.

Wrapping Up

A well-organized Chart of Accounts is fundamental to successful financial management. By understanding its role and carefully customizing it to match your business activities, you create a solid foundation for all your accounting work in QuickBooks Online. Not only does this structure lead to more accurate financial reporting and smoother tax preparation, but it also provides valuable insights that can guide strategic decisions.

As you continue through this guide, you'll see how the customized Chart of Accounts integrates with other elements of QuickBooks Online, making it easier to manage your income, track expenses, and ultimately, drive your business toward success. Now that you have the tools to set up and personalize your Chart of Accounts, you're well on your way to mastering the art of efficient, effective accounting.

CHAPTER FIVE

Managing Sales and Customers

Welcome to Chapter 5, where we focus on the lifeblood of your business—sales and customer management. In this chapter, we'll guide you through creating invoices and sales receipts, effectively managing your customers and products, and setting up recurring invoices to automate your billing process. These skills will help you streamline your sales process, reduce administrative work, and build stronger relationships with your customers.

Creating Invoices and Sales Receipts

Invoices and sales receipts are more than just documents— they're essential tools that facilitate cash flow and maintain a professional image.

- **Crafting Professional Invoices:** QuickBooks Online makes it easy to create clean, professional invoices that reflect your brand. You can include your logo, customize color schemes, and adjust layouts so that every invoice feels uniquely yours. This personalization not only reinforces your brand identity but also instills confidence in your customers.

- **Capturing Sales Receipts:** Sales receipts are perfect for transactions that are completed immediately. They provide a quick record of the sale, confirming that the payment has been received. Whether you're selling online, in-store, or at events, sales receipts keep your records accurate and up-to-date.

- **Step-by-Step Guidance:** With intuitive prompts, QuickBooks Online guides you through each step—from selecting the customer to entering the products or services sold and finalizing the payment details. This process minimizes errors and saves time, ensuring that your financial data is always accurate.

- **Integration with Payment Gateways:** By integrating with popular payment processors, QuickBooks Online can streamline the invoicing process further. Customers can pay directly through a link on the invoice, reducing delays and making it easier for you to receive funds promptly.

Managing Customers and Products

A well-organized system for managing customers and products is key to keeping your business running smoothly.

- **Building a Customer Database:** Start by creating a comprehensive customer list. Record essential details such as contact information, payment terms, and purchase history. This organized approach allows you to quickly locate customer records and understand their buying patterns, which is invaluable for targeted marketing and customer service.

- **Product and Service Catalog:** Whether you sell physical products, digital goods, or services, having a well-maintained catalog within QuickBooks Online can simplify the sales process. Add detailed descriptions, pricing information, and categories for each item. This not only speeds up invoice creation but also ensures consistency in how your offerings are presented to customers.

- **Tracking Sales History:** QuickBooks Online automatically tracks transactions linked to each customer and product. With this historical data, you can analyze trends, identify top-performing products, and even forecast future sales. Understanding these trends allows you to make informed decisions about inventory and marketing strategies.

- **Customer Communication:** Efficient management means keeping lines of communication open. Use QuickBooks Online to send follow-up emails, reminders, or promotional offers directly to your customers. This ongoing engagement can build loyalty and encourage repeat business.

Setting Up Recurring Invoices

For businesses with regular, predictable billing cycles, recurring invoices are a game-changer.

- **Automating Routine Billing:** Recurring invoices allow you to set up a schedule for billing regular customers. Whether you're charging for a subscription, a monthly service fee, or any ongoing expense, you can automate the process so that invoices are sent out automatically at the predetermined intervals.

- **Customizing Frequency and Terms:** QuickBooks Online lets you define the frequency—be it weekly, monthly, or annually—as well as payment terms for each recurring invoice. This customization ensures that your billing aligns perfectly with your cash flow and customer agreements.

- **Reducing Administrative Overhead:** Automating the invoicing process frees up valuable time that you can invest in growing your business. By reducing the need for manual entry and follow-up, recurring invoices help you minimize errors and ensure that no billing cycle is missed.

- **Enhanced Customer Experience:** Consistency in billing enhances the customer experience. Your clients will appreciate the reliability and professionalism of receiving invoices on time, every time. This reliability can lead to stronger, trust-based relationships and smoother transactions overall.

Wrapping Up

Managing sales and customer relationships efficiently is crucial for your business's financial health and long-term success. In this chapter, you've learned how to create and customize invoices and sales receipts, manage your customer and product lists, and set up recurring invoices to automate your billing process. These practices not only streamline your day-to-day operations but also enhance your professionalism and customer satisfaction.

As you continue to integrate these tools into your business, you'll find that the streamlined processes allow you to focus more on strategic growth rather than administrative tasks. In the next chapters, we'll build upon these fundamentals to explore managing expenses and vendors, tracking inventory, and further optimizing your QuickBooks Online setup.

Embrace these practices, and you'll soon see how effective sales and customer management can drive your business forward, one transaction at a time!

CHAPTER SIX

Managing Expenses and Vendors

Welcome to Chapter 6, where we shift our focus from sales to the other side of your business finances: expenses and vendor management. In this chapter, you'll learn how to record bills and expenses accurately, connect and manage your bank accounts seamlessly, and set up vendors for streamlined payments. By mastering these processes, you'll gain better control over your cash flow and build strong, efficient relationships with your vendors.

Recording Bills and Expenses

Handling expenses is not just about keeping the books balanced—it's about understanding where your money is going and ensuring every dollar is accounted for. Here's how QuickBooks Online helps you manage this vital aspect of your business:

- **Effortless Bill Entry:** QuickBooks Online allows you to record bills as soon as they come in. Enter details such as vendor name, due dates, amounts, and categories, so that each expense is properly logged. This not only simplifies your bookkeeping but also ensures that you never miss a payment.

- **Expense Tracking Made Simple:** Whether it's office supplies, utilities, or travel costs, every expense can be recorded with ease. By attaching receipts and relevant documents directly to each transaction, you create an organized archive that's easy to reference during tax season or financial reviews.

- **Real-Time Visibility:** Recording your bills and expenses in real time means you always have a current picture of your spending. This insight enables you to make informed decisions, adjust budgets on the fly, and plan for future investments with confidence.

- **Automation and Reminders:** Set up automatic reminders for due dates and recurring bills, so you're always ahead of your payment schedule. This automation reduces the risk of late fees and keeps your vendor relationships in good standing.

Connecting and Managing Bank Accounts

Integrating your bank accounts with QuickBooks Online is like giving your accounting system a direct line to your financial heartbeat. Here's how to make the most of this powerful feature:

- **Seamless Bank Integration:** Connect your bank accounts to QuickBooks Online with just a few clicks. This integration automatically imports transactions, saving you time on manual data entry. It's a smart way to ensure that every transaction, whether it's a deposit or a withdrawal, is captured accurately.

- **Streamlined Reconciliation:** With your bank feeds connected, reconciling your accounts becomes a breeze. QuickBooks Online matches your bank transactions with the bills and expenses you've entered, highlighting any discrepancies and helping you quickly identify and resolve issues.

- **Enhanced Financial Oversight:** By regularly reviewing your bank transactions alongside your recorded expenses, you gain a deeper understanding of your cash flow. This real-time oversight is crucial for spotting trends, managing budgets, and ensuring that your business stays financially healthy.

- **Security and Confidence:** The bank integration in QuickBooks Online uses robust encryption to protect your data. You can have peace of mind knowing that your sensitive financial information is safe, while you focus on managing your business more effectively.

Vendor Setup and Payments

Your vendors are essential partners in your business, and managing these relationships efficiently is key to maintaining smooth operations. QuickBooks Online makes it easy to set up and pay vendors, ensuring that every transaction is handled professionally.

- **Comprehensive Vendor Profiles:** Start by creating detailed vendor profiles in QuickBooks Online. Include contact information, payment terms, and historical data on past transactions. These profiles serve as a one-stop reference for managing all your vendor interactions.

- **Organized Payment Schedules:** With a clear overview of when bills are due, you can schedule payments with confidence. QuickBooks Online allows you to set up payment schedules, so you always know which vendors need to be paid and when, reducing the risk of late payments or missed deadlines.

- **Streamlined Payment Processes:** Once your bills are recorded, paying vendors becomes a simple task. Whether you choose to pay online, by check, or through another method, QuickBooks Online keeps a detailed record of each payment. This not only simplifies your financial tracking but also helps you build trust with your vendors.

- **Vendor Communication:** Efficient vendor management is about more than just payments—it's also about maintaining open communication. Use QuickBooks Online to send payment confirmations, resolve disputes, or negotiate new terms. A well-managed vendor relationship can lead to better credit terms, discounts, and a more reliable supply chain.

Wrapping Up

Managing your expenses and vendors is a cornerstone of effective financial management. In this chapter, you've learned how to record bills and expenses accurately, integrate your bank accounts for real-time financial oversight, and set up a streamlined system for vendor management and payments. These practices not only help maintain a healthy cash flow but also free you to focus on strategic growth and innovation in your business.

As you continue your journey with QuickBooks Online, remember that every expense recorded and every vendor paid on time contributes to the stability and success of your business. With these tools and strategies at your disposal, you're well-equipped to navigate the financial side of your operations with confidence and ease.

Let's move forward, building on this solid foundation as we explore even more ways to optimize your accounting practices in the chapters ahead!

CHAPTER SEVEN

Tracking Inventory

Welcome to Chapter 7, where we dive into the world of inventory management—a vital aspect for any business that sells products. Whether you're running an online store, a brick-and-mortar shop, or even a service-based business with tangible items, tracking your inventory accurately is key to maintaining profitability and ensuring customer satisfaction. In this chapter, we'll guide you through enabling and using the inventory feature in QuickBooks Online and walk you through creating and managing your inventory items.

Enabling and Using the Inventory Feature

Before you can track your inventory, you need to enable the feature in QuickBooks Online. This process might sound technical at first, but it's designed to be straightforward and user-friendly.

- **Activating the Feature:** QuickBooks Online includes an inventory tracking option that you can easily turn on from the settings menu. Simply navigate to your account settings, find the inventory section, and follow the prompts to enable it. This step is crucial, as it allows you to capture all the details associated with your products—from quantity on hand to cost of goods sold.

- **Understanding How It Works:** Once enabled, QuickBooks Online begins to track every movement of your inventory. This means that when you record a sale or a purchase, the system automatically updates your inventory levels. This real-time tracking provides you with an accurate snapshot of your stock, helping you avoid issues like overselling or running out of popular items.

- **Seamless Integration with Other Features:** The inventory feature works hand-in-hand with other elements of QuickBooks Online. For example, when you generate sales receipts or invoices, the related inventory quantities adjust automatically. This seamless integration ensures that all your financial records are in sync, reducing the risk of errors and simplifying your overall accounting process.

- **Gaining Insights Through Reports:** With the inventory feature active, you gain access to detailed reports that show trends, such as which items are selling well and which might need a promotional boost. These insights are invaluable for managing stock levels, planning reorders, and making informed business decisions.

Creating and Managing Inventory Items

Now that your inventory tracking is enabled, the next step is setting up and managing your inventory items effectively. This process is all about organization and clarity, ensuring that every product you sell is accounted for properly.

- **Setting Up Inventory Items:** Begin by creating detailed entries for each product in your inventory. For every item, you can input essential information such as:

  o **Item Name and Description:** Make it clear and descriptive so you can easily identify it later.

  o **SKU or Item Number:** Use a unique identifier to track each product efficiently.

  o **Cost and Sales Price:** Record both the purchase cost and the price at which you sell the item.

  o **Quantity on Hand:** Keep an accurate count of your current stock levels.

These details form the foundation of your inventory management system, ensuring that every transaction is recorded with precision.

- **Managing Inventory Levels:** As sales and purchases occur, your inventory levels will change. QuickBooks Online updates these levels in real time, but it's important to periodically review your stock to ensure everything matches up. Regular checks help you catch any discrepancies early on—whether due to miscounts, damages, or other factors—and take corrective action promptly.

- **Organizing Your Inventory:** Consider categorizing your inventory items to streamline management further. For instance, you might group products by type, supplier, or seasonality. This categorization not only makes it easier to locate specific items but also provides deeper insights when reviewing sales trends and making purchasing decisions.

- **Adjusting and Reordering:** Sometimes, inventory levels will need manual adjustments. QuickBooks Online allows you to adjust quantities if you discover discrepancies during a physical count. Moreover, by monitoring your inventory closely, you can set reorder points to ensure you never run out of high-demand products. This proactive approach is essential for maintaining smooth operations and satisfying customer demand.

- **Tracking Costs Over Time:** For businesses that deal with fluctuating costs, it's important to track how much you're paying for inventory over time. QuickBooks Online lets you record changes in costs and compare them against your selling price, providing insights into your profit margins and overall business performance.

Wrapping Up

Efficient inventory management is more than just a bookkeeping task—it's a strategic component of your business that directly impacts your customer satisfaction and bottom line. By enabling the inventory feature in QuickBooks Online and carefully setting up and managing your inventory items, you create a system that minimizes errors, improves cash flow management, and provides actionable insights into your sales performance.

Take the time to configure and review your inventory settings as your business grows. With accurate tracking and detailed organization, you'll be better equipped to meet customer demand, plan for seasonal trends, and make informed decisions about your stock.

In the next chapters, we'll continue exploring ways to optimize your QuickBooks Online experience, diving into areas such as payroll, banking, and more advanced financial management strategies. For now, celebrate the fact that you've taken a significant step toward mastering one of the most essential aspects of your business's financial health—your inventory. Enjoy the process, and let your newfound organization pave the way for continued success!

CHAPTER EIGHT

Payroll and Employee Management

Welcome to Chapter 8, where we tackle one of the most critical—and sometimes challenging—aspects of running a business: payroll and employee management. Managing payroll efficiently isn't just about processing paychecks—it's about building trust, ensuring compliance, and setting the stage for a positive workplace culture. In this chapter, we'll walk you through setting up payroll, paying employees and contractors, and handling payroll taxes and compliance, all within QuickBooks Online.

Setting Up Payroll

Setting up payroll in QuickBooks Online is your first step toward a streamlined and stress-free pay cycle. Here's how you can get started:

- **Getting Started Made Simple:** QuickBooks Online offers an integrated payroll solution designed to simplify the process. During the setup, you'll be guided through a series of easy-to-follow prompts that help you input essential details about your business, such as your company's legal name, address, and employer identification number (EIN).

- **Tailored to Your Needs:** Whether you have a few employees, multiple contractors, or a mix of both, QuickBooks Online allows you to customize your payroll settings to match your unique needs. You can define pay schedules, select direct deposit options, and even set up additional pay types like bonuses or overtime.

- **User-Friendly Interface:** The payroll setup process is designed with clarity in mind. You don't need to be a payroll expert to navigate through the setup screens. With clear instructions and helpful tips along the way, you'll be ready to process payroll in no time.

- **Integration with Time Tracking:** If your business tracks employee hours using QuickBooks or connected apps, this data can seamlessly feed into your payroll system, ensuring accuracy and reducing manual entry.

By taking the time to properly set up your payroll, you're creating a foundation that not only ensures timely and accurate payments but also builds trust with your team.

Paying Employees and Contractors

Once your payroll is set up, the next step is ensuring that your employees and contractors are paid accurately and on schedule. Here's how QuickBooks Online helps you manage this process:

- **Streamlined Payment Processing:** With a few clicks, you can process your payroll cycle. QuickBooks Online calculates deductions, taxes, and net pay automatically, so you can focus on confirming the details rather than crunching numbers manually.

- **Direct Deposit Convenience:** One of the standout features of QuickBooks Online payroll is direct deposit. This option ensures that employees and contractors receive their pay quickly and securely in their bank accounts. It also minimizes the hassle and potential errors associated with printing and distributing physical checks.

- **Handling Different Payment Scenarios:** Every business is unique, and sometimes you need to manage both salaried employees and hourly contractors. QuickBooks Online allows you to set up multiple pay types, making it easy to accommodate varying work arrangements. Whether it's a bi-weekly paycheck for full-time staff or a one-time payment for a freelance project, the system adapts to your needs.

- **Maintaining Clear Records:** Each payroll run generates detailed reports that show the breakdown of each paycheck, including gross pay, taxes, and deductions. These reports not only help you stay organized but also serve as a reliable record for future reference or audits.

By automating the payment process, QuickBooks Online takes much of the stress out of payroll management, leaving you free to focus on growing your business and supporting your team.

Payroll Taxes and Compliance

Handling payroll taxes and staying compliant with regulations can feel like navigating a maze. Fortunately, QuickBooks Online is designed to help you manage these complexities with confidence.

- **Automated Tax Calculations:** One of the major advantages of using QuickBooks Online payroll is its ability to automatically calculate federal, state, and local payroll taxes. This means that every deduction is handled accurately, reducing the risk of errors that could lead to fines or penalties.

- **Timely Tax Filings:** The platform not only calculates your taxes but also helps you keep track of important filing deadlines. Some versions of QuickBooks Online even offer the option to file your taxes electronically. With built-in reminders and detailed reporting, you're less likely to miss a critical deadline.

- **Compliance Made Easier:** Staying up-to-date with ever-changing tax laws and employment regulations is a significant challenge for many businesses. QuickBooks Online keeps you informed with regular updates, ensuring that your payroll processes remain compliant with current laws. This proactive approach minimizes your risk and helps you focus on running your business.

- **Support and Resources:** In addition to automated tools, QuickBooks Online provides access to a range of support resources. Whether you need help with a specific tax issue or guidance on setting up deductions properly, the support team and online resources are there to assist you every step of the way.

By leveraging these features, you can navigate the complexities of payroll taxes and compliance with confidence, ensuring that your business remains in good standing with regulatory authorities.

Wrapping Up

Managing payroll and employee relationships is a crucial element of building a successful business. In this chapter, you've learned how to set up payroll, process payments for employees and contractors, and handle payroll taxes and compliance with ease using QuickBooks Online. By automating these processes and maintaining accurate records, you free up valuable time to focus on strategic initiatives and the growth of your business.

Remember, effective payroll management isn't just about meeting deadlines—it's about creating a reliable, supportive environment for your team, fostering trust, and ensuring your business operates smoothly from the inside out. As you move forward, these practices will become a seamless part of your routine, setting the stage for a more efficient and thriving business.

Let's continue our journey into the world of QuickBooks Online, knowing that you now have a solid grasp on managing payroll and employee management. Your team's success is your success, and with these tools at your fingertips, you're well-equipped to lead your business into a prosperous future!

CHAPTER NINE

Banking Rules and Reconciliation

Welcome to Chapter 9, where we demystify one of the backbone processes of effective financial management—banking rules and reconciliation. In this chapter, we'll explore how to automate bank transactions, leverage bank feeds and matching, and perform monthly reconciliation in QuickBooks Online. Mastering these processes ensures that your financial records are accurate, up-to-date, and give you a clear picture of your business's cash flow.

Automating Bank Transactions

Imagine a system where your bank transactions flow directly into your accounting software, eliminating the need for manual entry. That's the power of automating bank transactions in QuickBooks Online.

- **Streamlined Data Entry:** By linking your bank accounts to QuickBooks Online, your financial transactions are imported automatically. This means deposits, withdrawals, and other transactions appear in your system without the need to re-enter them, reducing manual errors and saving valuable time.

- **Customizable Rules:** Automation becomes even more powerful when you set up banking rules. These rules help the system automatically categorize and process transactions based on criteria you define, such as vendor names, amounts, or transaction types. Over time, these rules become tailored to your business, streamlining the process further and ensuring consistency across your records.

- **Real-Time Updates:** With automated bank transactions, you're always working with the most current data. This real-time access allows you to monitor cash flow, track spending, and make informed decisions quickly— essential for staying agile in a dynamic business environment.

- **Reducing the Administrative Burden:** Automating bank transactions minimizes the administrative work of manual data entry, giving you more time to focus on strategic activities. With fewer chances for human error, your financial data becomes more reliable, paving the way for smoother month-end closing processes.

Bank Feeds and Matching

Bank feeds and matching are at the heart of ensuring that the data coming from your bank aligns perfectly with your recorded transactions in QuickBooks Online.

- **What Are Bank Feeds?** Bank feeds are the live connection between your bank account and QuickBooks Online. They automatically pull in your latest transactions, allowing you to see real-time updates of your financial activities. This integration is a game-changer for keeping your records current without extra effort.

- **The Matching Process:** Once transactions are imported, QuickBooks Online works its magic by matching these transactions with the entries already in your system. This matching process identifies duplicates, flags discrepancies, and ensures that every deposit, payment, or expense is accurately accounted for.

- **Customizing Your Matching Rules:** Similar to automating transactions, you can set rules that help the system recognize and match transactions based on your business-specific criteria. Over time, these rules adapt to the nuances of your operations, making the reconciliation process even smoother.

- **Enhanced Accuracy:** With bank feeds and matching, you reduce the risk of overlooked or misclassified transactions. This accuracy is crucial for generating reliable financial reports and for making sure your cash flow remains transparent and trustworthy.

Monthly Reconciliation

Monthly reconciliation is a vital practice that ensures your books accurately reflect your bank's records. This process helps you catch errors, prevent fraud, and maintain a clear picture of your financial health.

- **The Importance of Reconciliation:** Reconciliation involves comparing the transactions in QuickBooks Online with those on your bank statement. This step verifies that every entry is correct and that your recorded balance matches your bank's balance. Regular reconciliation is a cornerstone of sound financial management.

- **Step-by-Step Process:**

o **Gather Your Statements:** Start by retrieving your bank statements for the month.

o **Match Transactions:** Use QuickBooks Online's reconciliation tool to match each transaction imported via your bank feed with those recorded in your system.

o **Identify Discrepancies:** Any unmatched or erroneous entries are flagged, allowing you to investigate and resolve issues before finalizing your records.

o **Finalize the Reconciliation:** Once everything aligns, confirm the reconciliation in the system. This process not only gives you peace of mind but also creates a documented trail for future reference.

- **Regular Reviews and Adjustments:** Even with automated tools, discrepancies can sometimes arise due to bank errors, timing differences, or manual overrides. Regularly reviewing your reconciliation reports allows you to fine-tune your banking rules and ensure that your system remains accurate over time.

- **The Benefits of a Clean Reconciliation:** A monthly reconciliation builds confidence in your financial data. It sets a solid foundation for accurate reporting, smoother audits, and better decision-making. When you know your books are in order, you can focus on growing your business without worrying about hidden financial surprises.

Wrapping Up

Mastering banking rules and reconciliation is essential for maintaining accurate, reliable financial records. In this chapter, you've learned how to automate bank transactions to reduce manual entry, harness bank feeds and matching to keep your data current and precise, and perform monthly reconciliation to ensure your records align with your bank's statements. Together, these processes not only safeguard your business against errors and discrepancies but also free up your time to concentrate on strategic growth.

As you continue your journey with QuickBooks Online, remember that these practices are not just about numbers—they're about creating a trustworthy financial system that supports every decision you make. With a clear view of your cash flow and a reliable reconciliation process, you're well-equipped to steer your business towards sustained success.

Let's move forward, confident in the accuracy and integrity of your financial records, and ready to explore even more advanced features in the chapters to come!

CHAPTER TEN

Projects and Job Costing

Welcome to Chapter 10, where we delve into the art of managing projects and understanding job costing within QuickBooks Online. Whether you're juggling multiple client projects, managing a construction site, or running any business that relies on project-based work, understanding how to set up projects, track time and costs, and evaluate profitability is essential. In this chapter, we'll show you how to create and manage projects effectively, so you can optimize your resources, control expenses, and ultimately boost your bottom line.

Setting Up Projects

Every successful project starts with a solid foundation. In QuickBooks Online, setting up projects helps you organize your work into manageable segments, making it easier to track progress and allocate resources.

- **Creating a New Project:** Begin by defining the project in QuickBooks Online. Input key details such as the project name, client information, start and end dates, and any relevant notes. This step creates a dedicated workspace for all the transactions, time entries, and costs associated with that project.

- **Organizing Tasks and Milestones:** Think of your project setup as a roadmap. Break down the project into distinct tasks or phases, and set milestones to track progress. This clarity not only helps in planning but also enables you to forecast resource needs and deadlines more accurately.

- **Assigning Team Members:** If your project involves multiple team members, assign specific roles and responsibilities from the start. This way, you can easily monitor who is contributing to which part of the project, ensuring accountability and smooth collaboration.

By setting up your projects meticulously, you create an organized framework that makes it easier to monitor every dollar spent and every hour worked.

Tracking Time and Costs

Once your projects are set up, the next step is to track the time and costs associated with each task. This is where QuickBooks Online truly shines, offering you the tools you need to capture detailed project data.

- **Time Tracking Made Easy:** Use QuickBooks Online's time tracking features or integrate with compatible time-tracking apps to record the hours worked on each project. Whether your team logs time manually or through automated systems, having accurate time records is essential for billing and productivity analysis.

- **Recording Project Expenses:** Beyond labor, projects come with various costs—materials, subcontractors, equipment rentals, and more. Record these expenses as they occur and link them directly to the respective project. This detailed cost tracking gives you a clear picture of where your money is being spent.

- **Combining Labor and Materials:** The true power of job costing lies in understanding the full scope of expenses. By combining time entries with direct costs, you get a comprehensive view of what it takes to complete each project. This information is invaluable for setting realistic budgets and adjusting your strategies if costs begin to creep up.

- **Regular Updates:** Keeping your time and cost records updated in real time not only helps you monitor progress but also alerts you to any variances from your planned budget. Regular updates allow for proactive management, so you can address issues before they become major problems.

Accurate time and cost tracking transforms raw data into actionable insights, allowing you to make informed decisions throughout the project lifecycle.

Evaluating Profitability

After a project is completed, evaluating its profitability is key to understanding your business's financial health and planning for future projects.

- **Analyzing the Numbers:** With all your time and cost data in one place, QuickBooks Online can generate detailed reports that break down the profitability of each project. Compare your estimated budgets against actual costs, and measure the revenue generated against expenses incurred.

- **Identifying Profit Drivers and Drains:** Look for trends in your project data to determine which elements contributed most to profitability and which ones dragged costs down. This analysis might reveal that certain types of projects are more profitable, or that specific tasks consistently overrun their budgets. Such insights can guide your strategic decisions and pricing strategies moving forward.

- **Calculating Return on Investment (ROI):** Assess the overall return on investment by considering both direct financial outcomes and indirect benefits like increased client satisfaction or improved operational efficiency. ROI calculations help you decide where to invest your resources and which projects to prioritize in the future.

- **Feedback and Continuous Improvement:** Use your project profitability evaluations as learning opportunities. Gather feedback from your team and clients, and analyze what worked well and what could be improved. This iterative process not only enhances your project management skills but also strengthens your overall business strategy.

By rigorously evaluating the profitability of each project, you're not just closing the books on completed work—you're gaining critical insights that drive smarter decisions, optimize resource allocation, and ultimately contribute to sustained business growth.

Wrapping Up

Projects and job costing are much more than accounting exercises—they're strategic tools that empower you to manage complex work, control costs, and maximize profitability. In this chapter, you've learned how to set up projects efficiently, track every hour and every expense, and evaluate the financial performance of your work with precision. With these tools at your disposal, you can confidently tackle even the most challenging projects, knowing that every detail is captured and every cost is accounted for.

As you move forward, remember that effective project management is a continuous journey of planning, tracking, and refining. Each project provides a wealth of insights that can inform better decision-making and fuel future success. Embrace the process, and let the clarity and control of QuickBooks Online propel your business to new heights.

Let's continue our journey, armed with the knowledge to transform your projects into profitable ventures!

CHAPTER ELEVEN

Customizing Reports and Dashboards

Welcome to Chapter 11, where we unlock the power of data visualization and analysis in QuickBooks Online. In today's fast-paced business world, having the right financial insights at your fingertips is crucial. In this chapter, we'll explore how to customize key reports like Profit & Loss, Balance Sheet, and Cash Flow statements, create and schedule custom reports that work for your business, and use KPI dashboards to monitor the metrics that matter most.

Profit & Loss, Balance Sheet, and Cash Flow

Your financial reports are the heartbeat of your business, providing a clear picture of your overall financial health.

- **Profit & Loss Statement:** Think of your Profit & Loss statement as a story of your business performance over time. It details your revenues, costs, and expenses, giving you insight into how much profit you're making. With QuickBooks Online, you can customize this report by filtering dates, comparing periods, and even drilling down into specific income or expense categories. This level of detail helps you understand what's driving your profits—and where you might need to make adjustments.

- **Balance Sheet:** The Balance Sheet is like a snapshot of your business's financial position at a specific moment. It lists your assets, liabilities, and equity, helping you assess the stability and liquidity of your company. QuickBooks Online allows you to tailor your Balance Sheet report to focus on particular accounts or segments, giving you a clearer view of your financial standing and making it easier to spot trends over time.

- **Cash Flow Statement:** Cash is the lifeblood of any business, and the Cash Flow statement shows you exactly where your cash is coming from and going to. This report helps you manage day-to-day operations and plan for future growth. By customizing your Cash Flow report, you can highlight critical areas like operating activities, investing, and financing, ensuring you always have a firm grip on your liquidity.

Creating and Scheduling Custom Reports

Every business is unique, and sometimes the standard reports just don't tell the whole story. That's where custom reports come in.

- **Tailoring Reports to Your Needs:** QuickBooks Online lets you build reports that focus on the specific aspects of your business that matter most. Whether you're tracking marketing expenses, monitoring vendor payments, or analyzing project profitability, you can choose which data to include and how to present it. This customization makes your reports not only more relevant but also more actionable.

- **Scheduling for Regular Insights:** Don't wait until the end of the month to review your numbers. With scheduled custom reports, you can have important insights delivered straight to your inbox on a regular basis—be it daily, weekly, or monthly. This proactive approach helps you catch trends early, make informed decisions faster, and keep your finger on the pulse of your business operations.

- **Interactive and Shareable:** Custom reports in QuickBooks Online are interactive. You can click through data points to explore more details and share these reports with your team or accountant with ease. This collaboration ensures everyone stays aligned and informed, driving your business forward together.

Using KPI Dashboards

Key Performance Indicators (KPIs) are the metrics that really matter for gauging your business success. KPI dashboards in QuickBooks Online turn complex data into visual insights that are easy to understand at a glance.

- **Visualizing Your Business Health:** KPI dashboards display important metrics like revenue growth, expense ratios, profit margins, and more in one centralized view. These dashboards are designed to give you a quick snapshot of your business's performance, so you can spot potential issues or opportunities immediately.

- **Customizable Widgets:** One of the great benefits of KPI dashboards is that you can customize them to fit your business's unique needs. Choose which metrics you want to track, arrange them in a way that makes sense for you, and even drill down for more detailed information. This customization ensures that your dashboard is not just a pretty picture, but a functional tool that helps you steer your business in the right direction.

- **Real-Time Monitoring:** With real-time data updates, your KPI dashboard reflects the current state of your business. Whether you're checking in from the office or on the go, you'll always have the most up-to-date information at your fingertips, enabling swift and informed decision-making.

Wrapping Up

Customizing reports and dashboards in QuickBooks Online transforms raw numbers into powerful insights that drive your business forward. By personalizing your Profit & Loss, Balance Sheet, and Cash Flow reports, creating and scheduling custom reports, and leveraging KPI dashboards, you gain clarity, improve decision-making, and ensure that your financial strategy is always aligned with your goals.

As you continue your journey with QuickBooks Online, remember that these tools are designed to adapt to your evolving needs. The more you customize and interact with your reports and dashboards, the more attuned you'll become to the subtle signals your business sends every day. Embrace this powerful functionality, and let it be the catalyst for informed decisions, sustained growth, and long-term success.

Let's harness the power of data together—one custom report and one KPI at a time!

CHAPTER TWELVE

Budgeting and Forecasting

Welcome to Chapter 12, where we explore the powerful tools QuickBooks Online offers for budgeting and forecasting. Whether you're planning for a steady growth phase or anticipating seasonal fluctuations, creating detailed budgets and accurate forecasts is essential to steer your business toward success. In this chapter, we'll cover how to build budgets in QBO, compare your actual performance against your planned numbers, and share valuable forecasting tools and tips to help you predict future financial trends.

Creating Budgets in QuickBooks Online

A well-crafted budget is more than just a spreadsheet—it's a financial roadmap that guides your business decisions.

- **Getting Started:** QuickBooks Online makes it easy to start your budgeting process. Simply navigate to the budgeting section, choose the time period that aligns with your business goals, and begin inputting your projected revenues and expenses. Think of this as your financial blueprint, outlining where you plan to invest your resources.

- **Tailoring Your Budget:** Customize your budget to reflect the unique aspects of your business. You can create budgets for different departments, projects, or even specific product lines. By segmenting your budget, you gain a clearer picture of how each part of your business contributes to the overall financial picture.

- **Adjusting for Flexibility:** Budgets aren't set in stone—they're living documents that evolve as your business grows. QuickBooks Online allows you to revisit and adjust your budgets as new data comes in or as market conditions change. This flexibility is key to staying responsive in a dynamic business environment.

Comparing Actuals vs. Budget

Once your budget is in place, it's important to regularly compare your actual performance against your planned figures.

- **Tracking Your Progress:** QuickBooks Online offers built-in tools to help you measure your actual financial performance against your budgeted amounts. This side-by-side comparison helps you identify areas where you're overperforming or falling short, giving you the insights needed to make timely adjustments.

- **Identifying Trends and Variances:** Analyzing the differences between your actual numbers and your budget helps you understand underlying trends. Are expenses creeping up in certain areas? Is revenue consistently higher than expected? These variances provide clues that can help you refine your future budgets and operational strategies.

- **Making Informed Decisions:** By regularly comparing actuals vs. budget, you gain a real-time snapshot of your business's financial health. This practice allows you to quickly identify and address any issues—whether it's cutting unnecessary costs or capitalizing on unexpected revenue opportunities—keeping your business on track to meet its goals.

Forecasting Tools and Tips

Forecasting is about looking ahead and preparing for the future, and QuickBooks Online offers a suite of tools to help you do just that.

- **Leveraging Historical Data:** One of the most effective forecasting methods is to analyze historical financial data. QuickBooks Online makes it easy to pull past reports, which you can then use to identify patterns and project future trends. This historical perspective is invaluable for predicting seasonal fluctuations, growth rates, and potential challenges.

- **Using Built-In Forecasting Tools:** QuickBooks Online comes equipped with forecasting features that help you simulate various business scenarios. Whether you're planning for a new product launch or anticipating market shifts, these tools let you model different outcomes and make data-driven decisions.

- **Integrating External Data:** Don't limit your forecasts to just your internal data. Consider integrating external factors such as market trends, economic indicators, and industry benchmarks. This broader perspective can enhance the accuracy of your forecasts and help you prepare for both opportunities and challenges.

- **Continuous Improvement:** Forecasting is not a one-time event but an ongoing process. As you gather more data and refine your assumptions, revisit your forecasts regularly. Adjust your models based on real-world outcomes and evolving market conditions to keep your projections as accurate as possible.

- **Practical Tips:**

- **Start Small:** Begin by forecasting for a short-term period (like the next quarter) before expanding to annual forecasts.

- **Collaborate:** Engage your team in the forecasting process—different perspectives can help refine your assumptions and make your forecasts more robust.

- **Stay Agile:** Use your forecasts to inform decision-making, but be ready to pivot if the numbers indicate a significant change in your business environment.

Wrapping Up

Budgeting and forecasting are the twin pillars of effective financial management. By creating detailed budgets in QuickBooks Online, comparing your actual performance against your planned numbers, and leveraging forecasting tools, you're equipping your business with the insights needed to navigate both opportunities and challenges.

Embrace these processes as essential components of your strategic planning. With accurate budgets and reliable forecasts, you'll not only keep a firm grip on your current financial status but also chart a clear course for future growth and success. Each forecast you make and each variance you analyze is a stepping stone toward a more informed, resilient, and prosperous business.

Let's step confidently into the future, knowing that every number has a story—and with QuickBooks Online, you have the tools to tell it well.

CHAPTER THIRTEEN

Automating Workflows

Welcome to Chapter 13, where we explore how to make your life easier by automating repetitive tasks and streamlining your accounting processes. Automation isn't just about saving time—it's about reducing errors, freeing up mental space for strategic decisions, and ensuring consistency in your day-to-day operations. In this chapter, we'll dive into setting up recurring transactions, creating automation rules, and integrating QuickBooks Online with third-party apps like Zapier and Gusto.

Recurring Transactions

Imagine not having to manually enter the same data every week or month. Recurring transactions are designed to do exactly that, taking the repetitive tasks off your plate so you can focus on what truly matters.

- **What Are Recurring Transactions?** Recurring transactions in QuickBooks Online let you automate routine entries—like monthly invoices, rent payments, or subscription charges—so they're generated automatically on a schedule you set. This consistency not only saves you time but also ensures that important transactions never slip through the cracks.

- **Setting Up Recurring Transactions:** The process is straightforward. Within QuickBooks Online, navigate to the recurring transactions section, choose the type of transaction (such as invoices or bills), and configure the details. Set the frequency, add any specific terms, and even customize the template with your branding. Once set, the system takes care of generating these entries for you.

- **Benefits for Your Business:** Automating recurring transactions minimizes manual data entry and the potential for errors. It keeps your cash flow predictable and your books up-to-date, which is particularly valuable during busy periods or when you're managing multiple tasks at once.

Creating Automation Rules

While recurring transactions handle routine entries, automation rules in QuickBooks Online can take care of more nuanced, day-to-day activities. These rules are your opportunity to tailor the software to your specific workflow.

- **Understanding Automation Rules:** Automation rules are predefined criteria that instruct QuickBooks Online on how to process certain transactions. For example, you can set a rule that automatically categorizes expenses from a specific vendor or flags transactions above a certain amount for review.

- **Setting Up Your Rules:** Creating automation rules is like setting up your own personal assistant within QuickBooks. In the automation section, you can define conditions based on vendor names, transaction amounts, dates, or other relevant factors. Once the rule is saved, every transaction that meets the criteria is automatically processed according to your instructions—whether that means being assigned a particular category or marked for follow-up.

- **Tailoring to Your Workflow:** The beauty of automation rules lies in their flexibility. You can create as many rules as needed to streamline your operations, ensuring consistency and freeing you from repetitive tasks. This setup not only speeds up the reconciliation process but also makes your overall bookkeeping more accurate and reliable.

Integrating with Third-Party Apps

To truly unlock the power of QuickBooks Online, integrating with third-party apps can extend its capabilities and create a seamless, interconnected workflow. Apps like Zapier, Gusto, and others offer tools that can automate processes beyond basic accounting tasks.

- **Expanding Your Capabilities with Zapier:** Zapier acts as a bridge between QuickBooks Online and thousands of other apps, automating workflows across different platforms. For example, you can set up a Zap that automatically adds a new customer from your e-commerce platform to QuickBooks, or one that triggers an email reminder when an invoice is due.

- **Streamlining Payroll with Gusto:** For businesses that need a robust payroll solution, integrating with Gusto can simplify employee payments and benefits management. This integration allows you to synchronize payroll data between QuickBooks Online and Gusto, ensuring that your financial and HR records are always in sync.

- **Other Useful Integrations:** Depending on your business needs, you might also integrate with inventory management tools, CRM systems, or project management apps. Each integration is designed to reduce manual data transfers, improve accuracy, and provide you with a more comprehensive view of your business operations.

- **Setting Up Integrations:** The process typically involves connecting your QuickBooks account with the third-party app through secure API connections. Most of these integrations come with step-by-step guides, making it simple to set up and start benefiting from automated workflows that span multiple areas of your business.

Wrapping Up

Automating workflows in QuickBooks Online is about more than just saving time—it's about creating a more efficient, error-free, and agile business environment. By setting up recurring transactions, creating personalized automation rules, and integrating with third-party apps, you free yourself from repetitive tasks and pave the way for strategic decision-making.

As you continue to refine your processes, remember that automation is an evolving journey. Experiment with different rules, explore new integrations, and continuously adjust your workflows to match your business's changing needs. With these automation strategies in place, you're not just keeping up with the demands of modern business—you're staying one step ahead.

Let's embrace the power of automation together, so you can focus on growing your business and achieving the success you deserve!

CHAPTER FOURTEEN

Managing Taxes and Year-End Prep

Welcome to Chapter 14, where we tackle the often-daunting world of taxes and year-end preparations. Taxes can be complex and time-consuming, but with the right tools and strategies in QuickBooks Online, you can simplify the process and avoid last-minute stress. In this chapter, we'll guide you through configuring and reporting sales tax, managing estimated tax payments, and preparing for tax season with confidence, including collaborating effectively with your CPA.

Sales Tax Configuration and Reporting

Sales tax is a crucial element of your business's compliance and cash flow management. Getting it right ensures you meet legal obligations and maintain smooth operations.

- **Setting Up Sales Tax:** QuickBooks Online makes it easy to configure your sales tax settings. Start by entering the tax rates and rules applicable to your business—this might vary by state or even by local jurisdiction. With guided prompts, you can ensure that every transaction is tagged with the correct tax rate, so you never miss a filing.

- **Automated Tax Calculation:** Once set up, QuickBooks Online automatically calculates the appropriate sales tax for every sale. This automation minimizes errors and saves you from manual calculations, allowing you to focus on growing your business rather than crunching numbers.

- **Accurate Reporting:** Detailed sales tax reports in QuickBooks Online provide a clear view of the taxes collected and owed. These reports are invaluable during filing periods, giving you confidence that your data is accurate and ready for submission to tax authorities.

- **Staying Compliant:** Regularly reviewing your sales tax settings and reports ensures you stay up-to-date with any changes in tax laws or rates. This proactive approach helps avoid penalties and maintains a smooth relationship with tax authorities.

Estimated Tax Payments

Managing estimated tax payments is key to avoiding surprises when tax season arrives. QuickBooks Online provides tools to help you calculate and schedule these payments throughout the year.

- **Understanding Estimated Taxes:** For many small businesses and self-employed professionals, estimated taxes are a critical part of tax planning. Rather than waiting until the end of the year, making regular estimated tax payments helps distribute the tax burden evenly and prevents cash flow issues.

- **Calculating Your Payments:** QuickBooks Online can help you track your income and expenses to estimate your tax liability. By comparing your actual performance against your tax obligations, you can determine how much to pay each quarter. This data-driven approach takes the guesswork out of the process.

- **Scheduling Reminders:** The platform allows you to set reminders for upcoming estimated tax payments. With these alerts, you're less likely to miss a deadline, which is essential for avoiding penalties and maintaining good standing with tax authorities.

- **Adapting to Change:** As your business grows and evolves, your tax liability may change. Regularly reviewing your estimated tax calculations in QuickBooks Online ensures that you adjust your payments accordingly, keeping your finances in balance year-round.

Preparing for Tax Season and CPA Collaboration

When it comes to tax season, preparation is everything. With QuickBooks Online, you're equipped to compile all necessary data efficiently, making it easier to work with your CPA and file your taxes accurately.

- **Organized Financial Data:** One of the biggest advantages of QuickBooks Online is the centralized organization of your financial records. All your income, expenses, sales tax, and estimated payments are neatly compiled in one place, making tax preparation far less daunting.

- **Generating Detailed Reports:** Use the reporting tools in QuickBooks Online to generate comprehensive documents that summarize your financial activities over the year. These reports serve as the backbone of your tax return, providing your CPA with all the information they need to file accurately.

- **Collaboration with Your CPA:** A strong partnership with your CPA is key to a stress-free tax season. QuickBooks Online facilitates collaboration by allowing you to share access with your CPA, ensuring they can review your data in real time. This seamless exchange of information not only speeds up the process but also helps identify any discrepancies early on.

- **Year-End Checklist:** As you approach year-end, take advantage of built-in checklists and reminders in QuickBooks Online to ensure that all necessary tasks are completed. From reconciling bank accounts to verifying sales tax configurations, these checklists serve as a roadmap to a successful year-end close.

- **Planning for the Future:** Post-tax season, take time to review your financial performance and tax strategy. What worked well? Where can improvements be made? This reflective process not only prepares you for the next tax cycle but also helps you make smarter decisions for your business growth.

Wrapping Up

Managing taxes and preparing for year-end might seem overwhelming, but with QuickBooks Online, it becomes a systematic, manageable process. By configuring your sales tax settings accurately, staying on top of estimated tax payments, and preparing thoroughly for tax season with detailed reports and CPA collaboration, you set the stage for financial success and peace of mind.

Remember, taxes are not just a yearly obligation—they're an integral part of your business's financial health. With the right tools and a proactive approach, you can navigate tax season confidently, ensuring compliance, avoiding penalties, and positioning your business for long-term growth.

Let's embrace these strategies together, transforming tax time from a period of stress into an opportunity for clarity and strategic planning. Here's to a smooth tax season and a successful year ahead!

CHAPTER FIFTEEN

Time-Saving Tips, Common Pitfalls, and Data Security

Welcome to Chapter 15, where we bring together three essential components that empower you to work smarter, avoid common mistakes, and protect your financial data in QuickBooks Online. In this chapter, we'll share must-know hacks and keyboard shortcuts to speed up data entry, point out common pitfalls like reconciliation errors and duplicate entries, and guide you through setting robust data security and user permissions.

Time-Saving Tips and Keyboard Shortcuts

Time is money, and QuickBooks Online is designed to help you save both. Here are some practical tips to help you breeze through routine tasks.

Must-Know Hacks

- **Personalize Your Dashboard:** Customize your QuickBooks dashboard so that your most frequently used features are front and center. This simple tweak can reduce the time you spend navigating the software.

- **Batch Actions:** Whenever possible, use batch processing for common tasks like updating transactions or sending multiple invoices. This consolidation not only saves time but also minimizes the risk of manual errors.

- **Use Templates:** Save customized templates for invoices, estimates, and other documents. Once you set up your preferred format, you can reuse it for every transaction, ensuring consistency and cutting down on repetitive work.

Speeding Up Data Entry

- **Keyboard Shortcuts:** Familiarize yourself with QuickBooks Online's keyboard shortcuts. For example, use "Ctrl + Alt + I" to create a new invoice and "Ctrl + Alt + E" to enter a new expense. These shortcuts can significantly speed up your workflow.

- **Auto-Fill Features:** Take advantage of auto-fill functions where QuickBooks automatically populates recurring fields based on previous entries. This not only speeds up data entry but also helps reduce mistakes.

- **Smart Search:** Use the built-in search bar to quickly locate transactions, customers, or vendors. This feature streamlines the process of updating records or verifying information, allowing you to get things done faster.

Common Mistakes to Avoid

Even the best systems can be tripped up by a few common errors. Let's look at some pitfalls and how to avoid them.

Reconciliation Errors

- **Stay Current:** Reconcile your accounts regularly—ideally monthly. This habit makes it easier to spot and correct discrepancies early before they turn into larger issues.

- **Double-Check Entries:** Always verify that the amounts and dates of your transactions match your bank statements. Regular audits and a thorough review of your entries can help catch errors before finalizing your records.

Misclassified Transactions

- **Clear Account Structure:** Maintain a well-organized Chart of Accounts so that each transaction is easily and correctly classified. Take the time to review your account categories periodically to ensure they still align with your business needs.

- **Consistent Data Entry:** Establish clear guidelines for categorizing transactions and communicate these with your team. Consistency is key to preventing misclassifications that can skew your financial reports.

Duplicate Entries

- **Utilize Bank Feeds:** Rely on automated bank feeds and matching features to avoid duplicate entries. When QuickBooks Online automatically identifies duplicate transactions, investigate and resolve them immediately.

- **Regular Reviews:** Schedule regular reviews of your transaction history. Periodic audits can help you spot any duplicate entries and correct them promptly, ensuring your books remain accurate.

Data Security and User Permissions

Protecting your sensitive financial data is as important as managing it effectively. QuickBooks Online offers robust features to help safeguard your information.

Setting Roles and Restrictions

- **Define User Roles:** Establish clear roles and permissions for everyone who accesses your QuickBooks account. Not every user needs full administrative privileges.

Tailor access so that employees see only what they need to perform their jobs.

- **Custom Restrictions:** Use QuickBooks Online's customizable permissions to restrict access to sensitive data or specific functions. This minimizes the risk of unauthorized changes or data breaches.

Audit Trail and Backup Tips

- **Maintain an Audit Trail:** Enable and monitor the audit trail feature in QuickBooks Online. This detailed log tracks all changes made to your data, providing a clear record that can help identify any suspicious activity or errors.

- **Regular Backups:** Although QuickBooks Online automatically backs up your data, it's wise to periodically export your reports and key data sets for an extra layer of protection. Keeping local copies can be a lifesaver in the event of unexpected issues.

- **Stay Updated:** Always keep your software up-to-date to benefit from the latest security patches and enhancements. Regular updates help protect your system from emerging threats and vulnerabilities.

Wrapping Up

By integrating these time-saving tips, avoiding common pitfalls, and setting strong data security measures, you lay a solid foundation for efficient and secure accounting practices. Mastering keyboard shortcuts and automating routine tasks gives you more time to focus on growing your business, while vigilant data entry and regular reconciliations keep your financial information accurate and reliable. At the same time, robust user permissions and an active audit trail ensure that your data remains safe and secure.

As you continue using QuickBooks Online, remember that these practices are not just about working faster or avoiding mistakes—they're about building a resilient system that supports your business's growth and success. Embrace these strategies, and you'll find that managing your finances becomes a smoother, more empowering process.

Let's move forward with confidence, knowing that with each click and keystroke, you're enhancing your business's efficiency and safeguarding its future.

BONUS SECTION

Extra Value for Your QuickBooks Journey

As a special thank you for choosing this guide, we're excited to offer you three exclusive bonuses designed to accelerate your QuickBooks Online mastery and simplify your financial management. Each bonus is crafted with practical tips and ready-to-use tools that you can implement immediately to enhance your workflow, streamline setup, and ensure your financial documents look professional. Let's dive into the extra resources waiting for you!

Bonus 1: Quick Reference Cheat Sheet

Imagine having a handy guide right at your fingertips whenever you need to perform a quick task or troubleshoot a workflow. Our Quick Reference Cheat Sheet is designed to be exactly that—a compact, easy-to-use tool that helps you navigate QuickBooks Online like a pro.

- **Handy Shortcuts:** Discover a curated list of keyboard shortcuts and quick commands that speed up everyday tasks. From creating new invoices to navigating through different sections, these shortcuts save you time and make your workflow smoother.

- **Workflow Tips:** Alongside shortcuts, you'll find tips and tricks to simplify processes like reconciling accounts, setting up recurring transactions, and generating essential reports. Whether you're a beginner or an advanced user, these insights are here to keep you one step ahead.

- **Portable and Practical:** Print it out or keep it open on your device as a constant companion. This cheat sheet is a quick reference that ensures you never have to waste time searching for solutions—everything you need is in one place.

Bonus 2: 30-Day QuickBooks Setup Challenge

Setting up QuickBooks Online can feel overwhelming, but what if you had a daily roadmap to guide you through the process? Our 30-Day QuickBooks Setup Challenge is a step-by-step daily checklist designed to get your accounting system up and running perfectly.

- **Daily Checklist:** Each day, you'll tackle a specific aspect of the setup process—whether it's entering your business profile, configuring your Chart of Accounts, or automating workflows. This structured approach helps you build your system piece by piece, making the whole process manageable and stress-free.

- **Expert Guidance:** Along the way, you'll receive actionable tips and expert advice to ensure every step is completed correctly. The challenge is designed to empower you, so you build confidence in using QuickBooks Online while creating a customized financial management system.

- **Track Your Progress:** With a clear roadmap in front of you, it's easy to see your progress over the 30 days. By the end of the challenge, you'll have a fully configured QuickBooks Online account that's tailored to your business needs and ready for advanced operations.

Bonus 3: Exclusive Templates Pack

Consistency is key when it comes to professional financial documents. Our Exclusive Templates Pack provides you with a suite of customizable templates designed to give your accounting documents a polished, professional look right out of the box.

- **Invoice Templates:** Impress your clients with sleek, branded invoices that reflect your business identity. These templates are easy to modify—simply add your logo, adjust the colors, and update your information to match your brand.

- **Chart of Accounts Samples:** Get a head start by exploring sample Chart of Accounts setups that have been crafted for various industries and business sizes. These samples serve as a solid foundation, helping you organize your financial data effectively while saving you the time of building one from scratch.

- **Budget Templates:** Stay on top of your finances with ready-to-use budget templates. Whether you're planning a monthly budget or an annual forecast, these templates help you track expenses, monitor revenue, and keep your financial goals in sight—all while providing a clear structure for your budgeting process.

Wrapping Up the Bonus Section

These three bonuses are more than just add-ons—they're valuable tools designed to enhance every aspect of your QuickBooks Online experience. The Quick Reference Cheat Sheet empowers you with time-saving shortcuts and practical workflow tips. The 30-Day QuickBooks Setup Challenge turns the daunting task of setup into a manageable, day-by-day journey toward mastery. And the Exclusive Templates Pack ensures that your financial documents are both professional and personalized.

We hope these bonuses add significant value to your learning journey and help you unlock the full power of QuickBooks Online. Embrace these tools, integrate them into your daily routine, and watch how they transform your approach to managing your business finances. Enjoy the journey, and here's to your continued success!

CONCLUSION

As we reach the end of this comprehensive guide, it's time to reflect on the journey you've taken with QuickBooks Online. Whether you're just starting out or have advanced your skills to a new level, you now have a robust understanding of how to set up your books, streamline workflows, and leverage powerful tools that can drive your business forward.

Final Thoughts and Next Steps

You've learned how to:

- Configure your account and personalize your business profile,

- Master fundamental tasks like managing sales, expenses, and inventory,

- Leverage advanced tools for payroll, project costing, and customized reporting,

- And even automate routine tasks to save time and reduce errors.

These skills aren't just about managing numbers—they're about empowering you to make informed decisions, grow your business, and achieve financial clarity. Now is the time to put these insights into action. Take a moment to review the chapters that resonated most with you, and start applying those strategies to your daily operations.

Your next steps might include:

- **Revisiting key sections:** Refresh your understanding of complex topics like payroll setup or budgeting.

- **Implementing automation:** Explore setting up recurring transactions and custom rules to make your daily processes more efficient.

- **Engaging with your team:** Share what you've learned with colleagues and discuss how these practices can further streamline your operations.

Remember, every improvement you make, no matter how small, contributes to a more organized and efficient business.

Continuing Education Resources

Learning is an ongoing journey. To keep your QuickBooks skills sharp and stay updated on the latest features:

- **Explore Official Resources:** QuickBooks offers a wealth of tutorials, webinars, and support articles on their website.

- **Online Courses and Forums:** Consider enrolling in online courses or participating in forums and user groups where you can share experiences and ask questions.

- **Books and Blogs:** Keep an eye out for new publications and expert blogs that dive deeper into advanced accounting strategies and software updates.

By continuously seeking knowledge, you'll be able to adapt to new challenges and maximize the benefits of QuickBooks Online for your business.

Join the Community

You're not alone on this journey. The QuickBooks community is vibrant and supportive—full of entrepreneurs, small business owners, and accounting professionals who are eager to share their experiences.

- **Newsletter:** Sign up for our newsletter to receive regular tips, updates, and exclusive content that can help you stay ahead.

- **Facebook Group:** Join our Facebook group to connect with like-minded business owners, ask questions, and participate in discussions. It's a great place to exchange ideas, celebrate successes, and learn from one another.

- **Other Platforms:** Follow us on social media and participate in webinars and live Q&A sessions. These platforms are perfect for staying engaged, gaining new insights, and continuously improving your financial management skills.

Your active participation in the community not only enriches your own experience but also contributes to a collective pool of knowledge that benefits everyone.

In Closing

Thank you for taking the time to invest in your financial literacy and business growth by exploring this guide. With the comprehensive strategies, practical tips, and bonus resources provided, you are now equipped to harness the full power of QuickBooks Online.

Embrace the journey ahead with confidence and curiosity. Every step you take towards mastering your financial tools is a step towards achieving greater success. We're excited to see where this newfound expertise takes you, and we're here to support you every step of the way.

Here's to smarter management, more efficient workflows, and a future of growth and success!

Happy bookkeeping!

www.ingramcontent.com/pod-product-compliance
Lightning Source LLC
LaVergne TN
LVHW052056060326
832903LV00061B/983